How ONE Choice Directs Your

Destiny

The Book of Truth
Introducing Mind Interpretation Theory

by

Dr. Edmond Kelly Jr.

Published by Dr. Edmond Kelly Jr.
P.O. Box 88442
Carol Stream, IL. 60188
edkelly119@gmail.com

Distribution by www.Createspace.com and www.Amazon.com
Printed in the United States of America
ISBN-13: 978-1542996679 (CreateSpace-Assigned)
ISBN-10: 1542996678

Library of Congress to catalogued the original edition as follows:
How One Choice Directs Your DESTINY: The Book of Truth introducing Mind Interpretation Theory
Application: Psychology / Developmental / Lifespan Development
Biblical references are from King James and New King James versions.

Cover design by Dr. Edmond Kelly Jr.

Special Thanks to the guest editors: Shunika Michelle Johnson and Toya D. Sledd

ISBN: 1542996678
ISBN-13: 9781542996679

TO MY FAMILIY...

I
dedicate
this
book
to
where
it
all
began.
Pops,
thank
you

for being the great WARRIOR you
are.
I
am
your son, your son forever.
Mother
Dear
you
have
shown
me
.unconditional :is LOVE true what

Lisa
thank
you
for
being
the
best
big
sister
of
Sisters.
Your
STRENGTH

has taught me that to overcome is
not a
dream
but
reality. Shawn, my sister of
sisters.
It was
your
passion
of
SUCCESS
that
.Excellence towards me pushed

From "Maywood" Ed to Dr. Kelly. Thank you for always loving me as Scampi

CONTENTS

First Fruit Foreword...pg. 7

Acknowledgments..pg. 8

Laughter and tears for so many years, but now I am aware. Thank you, God for

bringing me here...pg. 11

INTRODUCTION

Welcome to Your New Beginning.............................pg. 12

Truth..pg. 15

My Prayer of Truth...pg. 16

If your truth is to set me free, then free my truth to decide the best in

me..pg. 17

1   *EXPLORATION OF ONESELF*...............................pg. 18

Who I am?

Three Simple Questions.......................................pg. 19

1. How did your life influence me?
2. Who was I as your child?
3. Which parent do I act more like?

Significance of the three questions...........................pg. 21

You're not alone in the journey of knowing who you are............pg. 23

Moses to know himself for us..pg. 24

"To Get mine, Get in line"..pg. 26

Exploration of Oneself Reflection Exercise...........................pg. 30

I am all-knowing, but know-nothing..pg. 34

2   *S.O.S. PLAN*...pg. 35

What is the S.O.S. plan?..pg. 36

The Breakdown of the S.O.S. plan..................................pg.36-37

    1. 'S': Stagnant

    2. 'O': Ongoing

    3. 'S': 'S'ome' I'gnorant 'N'ucklehead

S.O.S. plan examples..pg. 38

S.O.S. plan Reflection Exercise......................................pg. 45

From knowing oneself, to becoming intellectually sound. Twelve steps to keep you on the ground...pg. 48

3 **SPIRITUAL DIRECTION OF REMOVING YOUR THEN, TO MOVING FORWARD TO NOW**..pg. 49

Planting seeds..pg. 49

    1. Are you a farmer that plant seeds with love?

    2. Are you a farmer that plant seeds with discord?

    3. Are you a farmer that tills the soil with no seeds?

Twelve steps to keep you on the ground..............................pg. 51

Twelve Spiritual Direction of Inspiration............................pg. 54

Spiritual Direction of removing your THEN, to moving forward to NOW Reflection Exercise...pg. 69

Closure of the Book of Truth...pg. 76

SCRIPTUAL INDEX..pg. 78

ABOUT THE AUTHOR...pg. 80

My First Fruit Offering to YOU...

Proverbs 3:9-10

[9] Honor the LORD with your possessions,

And with the FIRST FRUITS of all your increase;

[10] So your barns will be filled with plenty,

And your vats will overflow with new wine.

I would like to thank God who has guided me to where I am today. In biblical times, the First fruit offering was given to God as a way of saying thank you, or giving Him your "first harvest" of the seeds that He has blessed you with. Before you begin this journey, I offer the first fruit in prayer:

Lord, thank you for all the blessings that you have bestowed upon my life. Not fully understanding why, I am here, or why you made me the way I am; You kept me in Your arms from the point of conception to now. Father, I am not perfect by any means. I am not the most spiritual, heavenly, kind-hearted, or the best Christian person, but I thank you for accepting me regardless of my faults. Thank you for not giving up on me. I have made mistakes; by myself and with others and you still allowed me to see one more day. In Jesus name, thank you for believing in me. Thank you for saving my soul, because without you, I would be nothing. I will do my best and place more effort into the life you have given me. Lord, purify my soul so that I can be humbled, spiritual, and untarnished. Help me remain a God-fearing person so I can provide the eternity of peace on earth as it is in heaven. I will praise you forever and in the Father, the Son, and the Holy Spirit, in Jesus name, Amen.

ACKNOWLEDGMENTS

First, I would like to thank God for making the pathway possible. It was His allowance that gave me strength, knowledge, and wisdom to create a book that will continue His blessings. To all that have and have not supported me from childhood until today. I appreciate every second and encounter with you. Whatever your feelings, thoughts, or actions towards me, you blessed me regardless.

To my beautiful wife, Felicia and children Zoey and Elicia. It was you all as one in faith that helped me when I was at my weakest point in life. Believing in me to complete this book, is what kept me strong. It was your strength and love that pushed me to be better, to be whole, and to know you will always stand by me. Felicia, thank you for starting my path of excellence. Sweetpea, thank you for loving daddy despite many days I was away, and Jellybean, thank you for recognizing daddy as your best daddy in the world. Felicia, I don't have any money and to the, THE SweetBean Express...always know that daddy will love you forever and we are all connected as one.

To my extended children; Audrianna, "my Audie"; your love has genuinely made many of my days better. Liam "T.J./Meatball". Thank you for always bringing joy to my spirit. Eden "lil Ed"; as you start your journey of life, know that your spirit has been made stronger because of you. To Kelsey and Reka, "THE original babies"; your birth created my lifelong campaign of willing to achieve more and both of you surpassed me years ago, just because you loved me always. All I wanted from you both was to succeed, never back down from what you wanted, and always be a blessing to life, which you both have done. So, with your love combined, thank you to, THE LilSweetbigbabiesMeatballAudieBean Express.

Mother dear and Pops...thank you for my life and helping me become a man. Shawn and Lisa, my sister of sisters…through any obstacles, we've stood strong, because you are great strong women. Mr. & Mrs. Jackson…for twenty years, it was your welcome into your home that created my destiny with you as my family. Auntie Sista', you are the wise in wisdom. My talks with you propelled my understanding of life to be far greater than I could imagine. Ms. Helen and Mr. Anderson…you both have given me a protected life as you raised me as your own. Tywayne, Mia, and Eden….my Siamese twin brother, thank you for thirty plus years of friendship, marrying your beautiful wife and even more beautiful child. Quondayln…you accepted me in a place of fatherhood for Audie and as your family. Brian, Ebony, Neffew, and Neicee…thank you for being the rock I needed. Apostle Hill, Deneen, and my CFKM family, thank you for keeping Christ in my life and trusting me to go beyond who I am as a Godly man.

To my friends, who are my family: Jason, Norman, Shanna, Big Tim, Emmalee, Giselle, Martia & Natasha, Tieshea, Christina, Chantel, Brandi, Nick, Pat, Roy & Mary, Mike & Karen, and Lisa & Javier, and your families. You guys have been with me since, "Ed Kelly" was just Edmond. Thank you, guys for never leaving my side and not last at all.

Toya Sledd, you have made this dream come true. It was your tireless effort that made this book and other endeavors possible in my life. Thank you for being who you are. I pray that you realize one day you are a mighty woman of God and cannot be stopped unless you stop yourself. From God, mom and through me, I pray you recognize that this moment is an accomplished moment for you. You, Toya Sledd have helped me Crossover From Death To Life…

To those who passed on who instill life in me…Uncle Curtis Kelly, Uncle Andrew Kelly, Mr. Waters, Thomas Belford, Monica Easton. I will always miss you and cannot wait for us to be together again.

Please forgive me in advance if I do not mention you now. Mentioning everyone would be too difficult to accomplish in one acknowledgement, because there are so many persons in my life who helped me be who I am today. I have several more books coming out and I'll get you at that point.

Laughter and tears for so many years, but now I

am aware.

Thank you, God for bringing me here

INTRODUCTION

Welcome To Your New Beginning

If you had one chance to seek the right path for your life, would you take it? People find themselves seeking ways to live a prosperous life, but never figure out their purpose in life. Over the years, men and women have learned that, "If you don't succeed, try, try again," but if you don't have a plan, "trying" will only constitute as failing. How do I know? I was that person. My "gut" told me I was going down the wrong path, which was the path of destruction that I accepted. My principles didn't have a solid plan, or purpose with life. If I did have a plan, it was based on the daily horoscope, or from someone who did not have my best interest at heart. For years, I was lost. I knew my life was in the direction of extinction, until I accepted Christ into my life. It wasn't until then that my life felt as if it rose from the ashes like the Greek mythological bird, "The Phoenix", preventing my life to continuously drift in hopelessness and despair. This rebirth led me to understand my purpose and plan in life, which is to help others find their own rebirth; their own Phoenix and to create a lifelong foundational theory that will change the outlook of your everyday decision making. The theory is called Mind Interpretation theory. M.I.T. is about trusting your gut, or spirit within you, gaining control of your mind, and making the right choices that will allow you to have a successful life. To achieve a "successful" life two things must occur within your thoughts. One, believe that success is based on what is accomplished and not measured by someone else standards. Two, learn to no longer live life in grey areas.

According to M.I.T., grey areas happen when the direction of the mind, or its thoughts, are allowed to remain in a state of non-existence. This grey area of life represents living in an empty space without meaning. Have you ever dated a person just because you had nothing else better to do? If so, what was the purpose; why did it happen, or more importantly, how was the outcome? Obviously, there was no purpose and most likely resulted as a complete waste of time for both of you. Imagine that you are driving a car on a nice summer day with your significant other and someone wants to stop for food. You have two choices: stop for food, or keep driving. There is no grey area. Sure, the decision is to think about whether you should stop or go, but ultimately, you have to make a decision. It's either you turn left, or turn right to get to your destination.

Is it true that our society lives in a grey area? Yes! This could be for any number of reasons, but one must realize that life is made up of the choices we make. In revelation 3:15-16 it says, *"I know your works, that you are neither cold, nor hot. I could wish you were cold, or hot. ¹⁶ So then, because you are lukewarm, and neither cold, nor hot, I will vomit you out of My mouth."* In this passage, the Bible mentions the complexity of a person's decision making. It could be hot, meaning: righteousness, cold, meaning: wrongful-doing, or lukewarm, meaning: living a life undecided or (grey area). Even the part, "I will vomit you out of My mouth entails the consequences of living in grey areas, which could be possible rejections of not making any righteous decisions. Outliving the grey areas, making righteous decisions and setting life in a direction of growth begin with understanding the truth.

The truth is knowing oneself, learning to avoid making irrational plans and being placed in a structured direction. At the end of each chapter there will be a reflection section with questions to help determine the idea plan for any decisions in the future. You will start each *Chapter Reflection* with prayer, or positive words. This will set the atmosphere with your thoughts as a preparation to answer the questions with honesty, direction, and understanding. The questions will only relate to the corresponding chapter that you have finished reading. If needed, go back and review the chapter to understand any question. It is very important to answer the questions as best as possible to prepare your destiny. Ideally, if a person begins to accept the truth of their life and place trust in God, our decisions will lead to success and many assignments will be fulfilled in triumph. I pray that this book will be that help guide for you to live more of an abundant life and not live a life that will steal your joy and ultimately destroy yourself. (John 10:10).

TRUTH

My Prayer for Truth

Heavenly Father, as I begin this path you have set before me, I want to say thank you. Thank you for the hard times and the misunderstandings I once had in my life. I know I may have wasted, misused, and mistreated the life You gave me as if it had no importance to me, but You gave me another day to see how great my life really is. I believe my life can be better. My Lord, help me believe in something more than what I know now. People say you know the truth, but it is difficult for me to find truth in something I cannot see. Show me how to find the truth in Your word. Lord, if the truth will set me free, I am asking for the truth now. I am ready to receive it so that I can be better and do better. In Jesus name, Amen.

If Your truth is to set me free, then free my truth

to decide the best in me

CHAPTER One...
EXPLORATION OF ONESELF

Who I am?

To gain understanding of oneself, one must identify his, or her attributes, strengths, interests, and most importantly, their values to structure your spiritual path. Various actions such as attaining feedback from others, examining your family history and completing spiritual assessments will provide insight not only into yourself, but help you make important life decisions. Your spiritual path is solely based on choice. You must ask the question, who am I? We should not to dwell on what happened yesterday, because we cannot change what we have lost. We must focus on today and start the process of living life more richly. Mark 11:24 says, *"Therefore, I say unto you, what things soever ye desire, when ye pray, believe that ye receive them, and ye shall have them."* In an effort to live in a grey-free zone, you must answer three simple questions to prepare for your life's principle, purpose and plan.

You can start with someone who knows your childhood. To learn about myself and my family background, I started with my parents. Be aware that when you take on this journey the conversation may be good, bad and extra ugly. Be mindful that your parent, guardian, or loved one may, or may not like your reason for questioning them. If you find it difficult to ask your parents, or those who have raised you, it's okay. Your questions and the conversations can easily be misconstrued as if you're questioning their integrity and judgment. This is vital to understanding "Who am I?" When I took this journey, I developed three questions to guide my conversations with my parents, so these same questions will be your guide when you converse with your family. Very briefly, I will provide you a summary of the answers to these questions that I used for myself. These questions will help begin the process to better control your destiny.

Three Simple Questions

1. How did your life influence me?

By hearsay, my parents did not get along at times. My father was a very funny, loving, All-American dad who was always there for his children. He is labeled as an, "All-American Dad" because he always fought until he could not fight any more for his children, even when he felt his manhood was being tested. There was another side to my father that I could not understand. One minute he was the "All-American Dad" and the next he was a malevolent man with strong and a sporadic callous side of him. The time before my parents divorced, the household had a real funky and negative vibe. I remember days before my parents' separation, the last meal we ever had as a whole family was on Sunday. Afterwards, my mother began to pack her belongings along with me and my sister's. In the living room, my father sat on the couch crying. He said, "I am sorry. Don't leave me. Don't take my kids away from me." That had to be one of the worse moments in my life that shaped my comprehension of why my family was so important and the impact of our choices; our decisions.

2. Who was I as your child?

I was a rambunctious young lad that enjoyed a carefree and happy life with cotton candy fields. Man, please! My nickname is Scammpppi and according to my parents, that nickname was used to stop me from doing whatever I was getting into at the time. Yes, my nickname was based on how I would get into a lot of things quickly like a mouse. Besides being a hellion to society, my parents said for the most part, I was a good kid with lots of energy. I have always had a good heart and loving spirit, but there was no stopping me from doing what I wanted to do. Now what is interesting is that my father said I was a follower, but my mother said I was a leader. At first, it was weird to hear two different perspectives of how I was as their child. One common statement they both shared was that I was a loner. I didn't need to be around tons of people to be happy, because I found happiness within me. After hearing that, I saw why making decisions was an easy transition for me from my parents making decisions for me.

3. *Which parent do I act more like?*

Out of my three questions, this had to be one of the most important, but funny question I asked. Why? Well, my parents, as crazy as they are, both said I am like the other parent. There was no grey zone. Between both of their explanations, it was very clear that I act more like my mom, especially in reference to why I make decisions the way I do. My "mother dear" has been the "loner" type. She has been in long lasting relationships, but with very weird living arrangements. One man she dated for over twenty years, and never married. They lived in the same house and had their own separate bedrooms. Really?! Even with her current boy toy, he is only allowed to visit when she chooses to see him. My mother is a very beautiful woman and could have men knocking down her door. Yet, she has always been known as the loner in her own space; her own sanctuary of peace.

My father is the opposite. He is always in need of a companionship. As long as I can remember, he stressed out about dying alone and how no one wants to be around him. This was always funny to me. Not that he is afraid to die alone, but the need to be dependent on others. For years, my father was the kick butt and take names later type of guy. However, his relationships bombed because he was stubborn, or as some say, stuck in his own ways. He did everything on his own and never asked for anything, but let's be real. God is the top and not the bottom; the head and not the tail. The only one true living God, but even He asked man to help Him as His children. Psalm 37:5, *"Commit your way to the LORD, Trust also in Him, And He shall bring it to pass."* So, why would my father think he had to do everything by himself? I am not sure, but after my conversations with my parents, learning their positions on life and how and why they made their choices, I realized I am like my mother. I have a beautiful wife and two daughters. I love the company of them and jokingly speaking about losing my hair because of them, but I also enjoy being alone. I certainly wouldn't mind being alone so I can grow some hair back. Even as a child with two older sisters and a brother from another mother, I was by myself for the majority of the time until leaving for college. This made my idea of decision making simple. I am a loner. This helped me realize that there is no such thing as a grey area. There might be other reasons why you are able to make clear cut, or precise decisions, but your principles begin at home.

The significance of the three questions

After asking my parents those three questions, it provided a better idea of who I am. Learning how I am today and why I do certain things was almost prophetic. With a better understanding, I know to believe in myself. The direction I choose will lead me to my promised land. If you look at other theories, or ideas about the connection between the child and the parent, typically a person would believe that the child who has been raised by the "one" parent would emulate their habits the most. In my case, it wasn't true, because I didn't live with my mother until I came back from college. I lived with my father from birth until the age of twenty-one. With my father, there was always something different between us. When I had a chance to be with my mother, my life became much clearer. Without question, I love my Pops, but the interaction between my mother and I was connected, better, and easier. My mother may have believed differently, since she mentioned many times, "you act just like yo' father," but when it comes to decision making, I am my mother all the way. I have told others in the past about my father and mother. Through my testimony, I always ended by saying, "my father raised me, but my mother made me a man!"

At the end of this chapter, you will receive an assignment to reflect on what was shared. Here is your assignment: Ask your significant family member(s) the three questions, obtain your answers, and write your personal feelings about what was learned from the person you spoke with about your background. This is where you can release your past feelings. To release my feelings, I decided to write poems about my father and mother. If you do not feel the need, or is not comfortable writing something about that person, that is fine. In my case, I needed to do it, because I was harboring emotions. For my future to begin, I needed to let go of my yesterday. Here are examples of how to express those feelings as you begin your journey towards destiny.

My Daddy

Daddy you have been with me through thick and thin; through my good, bad, and even living a life of sin. Over the years, you have been with me as much as anyone can be; especially when I messed up in school, I had to average 2-3 beatings a week. When you got hurt and had no money, you never gave up and I love you for that. You could have quit and left and got strung out on crack. Not having a mother at home was a big struggle for me, but you said, "Get going, don't stop, and be all that you can be." You brought God into my life by taking me to church, even though I complained about waking up early Sunday mornings. I know now that with God in my life, I can never be hurt. I'm proud of you, I respect you, and I love you unconditionally; because Daddy, remember this, Father and Son will be forever eternally.

Mother Dear

This is a poem to the one I love and cherish. You taught me love, the way to live, and most importantly, to believe. I wish that I could be in a better place, to see your smile once more in the special way. If I could please have one more day. Just to hear you say that things are okay.

But as time passed on, now things have changed. I went away to school and left you to stay. Please forgive me for that one mistake; you are who I want for always.

Has anyone talked to my Mother? The one who gave me strength to carry on; she told me, never to quit, persevere and I love you. Thank you for blessing me with the faith to stay strong.

As you may have noticed, there is a clear contrast between my Pops and my Mother dear. My pops blessed me with the foundation of a house and my mother placed a mansion above it. My mother was a loner, but always straight to the point and believed in standing by her word. When my mother couldn't be there during my younger years, God embedded in me this scripture that represents my mother's absence; John 14:1-4, which says,

"Let not your heart be troubled; you believe in God, believe also in Me. ² In My Father's house are many mansions; if it were not so, I would have told you. I go to prepare a place for you. ³ And if I go and prepare a place for you, I will come again and receive you to Myself; that where I am, there you may be also. ⁴ And where I go you know, and the way you know."

After I learned about my background and my family's "iconic" history, it blessed me and led me to share my blessings with others through this book. As we wrap up why these three questions are significantly important (How did your life influence me? Who am I as your child? Which parent do I act more like?), I need you to pay close attention to what you are about to read next because it's so profound in preparing your destiny…

You're not alone in the journey of knowing who you are

If we based our lives on others, the concept of taking another person's life and claiming it as yours, how can you become that person God has designed you to be? What is great about going through the process of learning who you are, is becoming more confident and knowing that others have walked a similar path to reach their destiny. Even great biblical leaders had difficulties accepting who they were in life and uncertain about their purpose. The mighty Moses was prophesized to free the Israelites from Egyptian ruler ship. Initially, Moses didn't know who he was, or God's true plan for his life. Moses would have been a great example to apply the "Who am I" technique by asking those three questions.

Moses to know himself for us

In the story of Moses, you will learn that he was given a leadership role from God to assist the Israelites out of bondage to freedom. In Exodus 3:9-15, the Israelites' story of captivity was told, but it also explained the maturation of Moses accepting his "Who am I," moment and God's plan for his life. Exodus 3:9-15(NKJV) says:

⁹ Now therefore, behold, the cry of the children of Israel has come to Me, and I have also seen the oppression with which the Egyptians oppress them.

¹⁰ Come now, therefore, and I will send you to Pharaoh that you may bring My people, the children of Israel, out of Egypt."

This is the crucial part of understanding, Who Am I

¹¹ But Moses said to God, "Who am I that I should go to Pharaoh, and that I should bring the children of Israel out of Egypt?"

Moses lacked understanding, confidence, and will

¹² So He said, "I will certainly be with you. And this shall be a sign to you that I have sent you: When you have brought the people out of Egypt, you shall serve God on this mountain."

¹³ Then Moses said to God, "Indeed, when I come to the children of Israel and say to them, 'The God of your fathers has sent me to you,' and they say to me, 'What is His name?' what shall I say to them?"

Moses receives confirmation of Who he is

¹⁴ And God said to Moses, "I AM WHO I AM." And He said, "Thus you shall say to the children of Israel, 'I AM has sent me to you."

Moses understands that Who he is, which is of His father, God.

¹⁵ Moreover God said to Moses, "Thus you shall say to the children of Israel: 'The LORD God of your fathers, the God of Abraham, the God of Isaac, and the God of Jacob, has sent me to you. This is My name forever, and this is My memorial to all generations.

Moses With Confidence understands who he is, knows his purpose, and is able to make historic decisions as a Leader. Now this is not to say that Moses all of a sudden was perfect after receiving his revelation of being like God, because Moses regressed back to questioning God of whom Moses was In Exodus 4:10-12:

"¹⁰Then Moses said to the LORD, "O my Lord, I am not eloquent, neither before, nor since You have spoken to Your servant; but I am slow of speech and slow of tongue."

¹¹ So the LORD said to him, "Who has made man's mouth? Or who makes the mute, the deaf, the seeing, or the blind? Have not I, the LORD?

¹² Now therefore, go, and I will be with your mouth and teach you what you shall say."

As you read Exodus 3:9-15 and Exodus 4:10-12, Moses spoke with a speech impediment. His words were stuttered, which he equated to not having intelligence. Even though we are created in God's image, like Moses, we oftentimes lose focus of accepting our role as a leader, husband, wife, son, daughter, friend, or colleague, because of the comfort of the grey area. It is very easy to conform towards lack of responsibility of making crucial decisions, but imagine where you, I, or Moses would be today if we didn't make those tough decisions.

After reading about Moses and understanding how it relates to our lives, you still may feel lost on knowing who you are. For you, I have created a special Dr. Kelly's rendition of how it became clear for Moses to accept his importance and destiny in life. Throughout this book, I will provide my perspectives, or interpretations of biblical stories, different accounts, and share my personal experiences. I hope you enjoy the Dr.

Kelly's rendition of the brief story of Moses called, *"To Get Mine, Get in Line"*

SCENE 1: TAKE 1

Moses: "Hey, God!

God: "Yes, Moses. What is it this time?"

Moses: "Well, do you remember back when you allowed my life to be sent down the river, washed ashore with the Egyptians and they raised me. But now I realize I am an Israelite and I need to go to the Pharaoh to, "let your people go."

God: "Yes, Moses.

Moses: "Well, not to be disrespectful, but I'm really not feeling that at all."

God: "Son, what are you talking about this time?"

Moses: "You see, God, Dad. I've been trying to figure out Who I am to the world, because I went from Israelite to Egyptian back to Israelite. Now you want me to tell the Pharaoh to stop tripping and let go of your other children. If you haven't noticed, I'm not the brightest apple in the bunch. I don't even talk, or walk right. I am so confused and lost right now."

God: "That's funny"

Moses: "What's so funny about that, Daddy God, God Daddy?" I'm trying to understand how I am supposed to get the Pharaoh to change his plans on building his kingdom and convince him to let EVERYBODY go? I mean, really God? You have to let me know what's really going on.

God: "Okay, son. You are very intelligent and wonderful. You should know this by now. Ask your sister Miriam. Do you remember your forefather Adam?

Moses: "Yes sir"

God: "He was created in the image of me, in the beginning which would be; let's see… ummm, yes! Genesis 1:27, "So God created man in His *own* image; in the image of God He created him; male and female He created them.""

Moses: "So what's your point, because I'm only seeing myself with my head chopped off as I'm still stuttering in front of the Pharaoh?

God: "My son. As you were created in my image and giving understanding as to Who "I" am. Recognize that Who "I" am is Who you are. It's true that you are not perfect, which is because of your extra great grandmother Eve, eating food that she wasn't supposed to eat, which is another story. But you are still created in greatness."

Moses: "So you're saying, I am You, but not completely because of my grandparents. However, I still have ruler ship to make mountains move because I'm like You?"

God: "EXACTLY! You are royalty. Not because you were raised as an Egyptian, but because you are my son. So, what I need you to do is know I love you and do what I ask you to do. There will be other times when you will question your authority, but know today, I am with you and in you."

Moses: "Daddy, I love you too! Let me go get my robe, garments and staff and get our people out of here."

Moses: Hey Dad?"

God: "Yes Moses?"

Moses: "Are you going to still do the staff trick thingy? It was kinda cool"

God: "MOSES, if you don't go! I swear, in My Son's name that you won't know about…

Moses: "Who?"

God: "Bye, Moses"

END SCENE

I hope you enjoyed the scene. Taking situations or telling stories from different perspectives can enlighten thoughts beyond what is written. Doing it this way helps to understand the context much easier and relate different perspectives to your personal journey. It can be quite difficult relating biblical truths to everyday life situations, which is why throughout this book series, you will read more renditions like, *"To Get Mine, Get In Line"*.

Conclusion

It is important to explore and learn more about yourself daily. This will strengthen your decision making and will guide you through a prosperous life. I hope that by sharing a glimpse into my family background and the exploration of my life provided insight for you. By exercising the three simple questions, you will learn about yourself and why it is critical to making straight forward decisions. You will allow your decisions to move beyond the grey areas of life and that "one-size-fits all" approach. The same decision for yesterday may not apply tomorrow. Your decision is based on: "It is what I SAY it is," and not, "it is what it is." The long-time cliché of, "it is what it is," is very much a living in the grey area. God gave us dominion. Genesis 1:26 says, "Then God said, *"Let Us make man in Our image, according to Our likeness; let them have dominion…"* Dominion is defined as to govern or rule. In Hebrew, the name is Râdâh, which means dominion, reign, to prevail against, and rule. God did not create man to rule indecisively. We are kings and queens by birth. We are created by God. Imagine Adam in the Garden of Eden in Genesis 2:19-20, taking on this responsibility [19] *"Out of the ground the LORD God formed every beast of the field and every bird of the air, and brought them to Adam to see what he would call them. And whatever Adam called each living creature, that was its name.* [20] Adam gave names to the cattle, birds of the air, and to every beast of the field," but was Adam indecisive? God created Adam with a directive mentality, therefore Adam couldn't be indecisive. If Adam was created with indirect decision making skills, can you imagine a lion being called a moose, or a chicken called a donkey? If a person said we are eating donkey for Thanksgiving and it looks like a chicken, you would look at them as if they were crazy. God created men and women with a clear understanding which is the same understanding we should use to direct our lives and make sound decisions. No grey areas, no maybes, or I don't know, because you really do know. A yes is a yes. The opposite of yes, whether it's a maybe, I don't know, or who knows, it will always be a no until you say, Yes! For those that live within the mental confines of the Stagnant Ongoing "S.I.N" (S.O.S.) plan, (which we will address in Chapter Two), I will make the point simpler and it's for sport lovers. Individuals must view their decision making as a coach. The team is down by three points and the coach must come up with a strategy to score within two minutes to win the game. What are you going to do? Go for a touchdown to win, or kick a field goal to tie? Either way, a decision must be made, because by having that indecisive mentality, you will lose time and the game. If you see life for what it is, pursue any given information to find a solution to the question and make your decision. This process will enlighten your individual path that was once unclear. You will begin to know who you are.

CHAPTER One...

Exploration of Oneself Reflection Exercise

Description of Exercise:

In chapter one, we looked into the idea of knowing oneself. The purpose was for you to learn the motives, understandings, and drives behind the way your decisions are made. After reading chapter one, we are going to use this time to reflect on any personal findings about yourself and how you have gotten better. Each exercise will start with writing a prayer/positive words of encouragement, and will be followed by questions that reflects what you have read during this chapter. For this to work, you must be completely honest with what was learned and tell your truth. Remember, *If Your truth is to set me free, then free my truth to decide the best in me.*

1. Prayer/Positive words of encouragement

_____

_____

_____

_____

_____

2. Who I am? Briefly describe who you are to yourself, then describe how you feel you are viewed by others.

_____

_____

_____

_____

_____

_____

3. Three Simple Questions.

These are the questions that you must approach your parents/guardians who raised you with. If you don't have parents/guardians to speak with, you can approach a sibling, relative, or friend who has known you for years. If those persons are not available, then look towards yourself in complete honesty to answer these questions. Remember, learning the truth about yourself will help learn more ways of making righteous decisions.

a. How did your life influence me?

_____

_____

_____

_____

_____

b. Who was I as your child, or as a child?

_____

_____

_____

_____

c. Which parent/relative do I act more like?

_____

_____

_____

_____

4. Briefly sum up your new found understanding of oneself.

_____

_____

_____

_____

_____

5. Release past feelings. For this exercise, you are to write a letter, poem, song, etc. to the person you have spoken to. If there were any misunderstandings, hurt, or mistruths, this would be the moment to release any negativity and start the process of moving forward.

_____

_____

_____

_____

_____

6. What was your Moses moment of feeling less than who you are?

_____

_____

_____

_____

_____

_____

7. Briefly sum up your thoughts and feelings from the reflection.

_____

_____

_____

_____

_____

_____

8. Close with prayer/positive words of accepting me

_____

_____

_____

_____

_____

_____

I am all-knowing, but know-nothing

CHAPTER Two...

S.O.S. Plan

Before I define the S.O.S. plan, let me first give you a brief history of the term. There was one man who always called me stupid for the things I did wrong, or looked wrong in his eyes. This man was my father. I could have turned on the shower to let it warm up and be called stupid. If I explained to him that I didn't know whatever information I was supposed to know, or didn't know, because he never told me. I was called stupid. Since I was his son, I was supposed to know it. One day I disagreed with his opinion on a business idea that would benefit my wife and children long after I was gone. He called me stupid, because I wanted to involve my wife in the decision-making process. Now you may be feeling sorry for me, but if it wasn't for the word, stupid, I would not have been able to share my experience and knowledge with you. It took me twenty years to overcome the hurt, pain, and disappointment. I thought my father did not appreciate me. At one point, I thought I would carry some generational curse that would be passed down from him to me, then to my children. Over the years, I have learned that even though a situation may seem bad, or disheartening, it is still a blessing. Let's look at 2 Corinthians 12:8-10:

8 Concerning this thing I pleaded with the Lord three times that it might depart from me.

9 And He said to me, "My grace is sufficient for you, for My strength is made perfect in weakness." Therefore, most gladly I will rather boast in my infirmities, that the power of Christ may rest upon me.

10 Therefore, I take pleasure in infirmities, in reproaches, in needs, in persecutions, in distresses, for Christ's sake. For when I am weak, then I am strong.

God taught me to take what is given and understand that all of it is a blessing because good will comes from it. If one person dies and one hundred people accept Christ as their Lord and Savior I will take that any day. Of course, the death of anyone, especially unexpectedly, is saddening, but if it meant one hundred lives are saved, then that infirmity turns into God's prosperity. My father calling me stupid for the most of my life (thank you Pops) *has led me to help hundreds more on how to avoid living on the S.O.S. plan. What is the S.O.S. plan?*

The S.O.S. plan is derived from and being called stupid. I took what my father rooted in me and made horrible, irrational decisions over a twenty-year span. I was a goofball without any principle, purpose, or plan. My father had an old school saying, "To just make it; By crook; or Hell in high water." In other words, just get the job done. Under the premise of just get the job done, the decisions I made affected my grades, relationships with girls, participation in sports, my overall maturity and becoming a man. Out of this, the Stagnant Ongoing "S.I.N." or S.O.S. plan was born.

The Breakdown of the S.O.S. plan

"S"

The first letter *"S"* stands for being Stagnant. Being stagnant allows us to not advance, or develop in the areas where we might struggle in. It may be in our marriage, our jobs, our children, or our love life, but we seem to become stagnant. Why? It could be because you are not willing to change, or afraid of growth. I know some, including myself, have been in that position, because changing would mean being uncomfortable and who wants to be uncomfortable? If our growth continues until we die, our stagnant state would prevent growth and cause us to spiritually die prematurely. You may say that the Bible teaches us to be steadfast, which is being stagnant. Well, I am here to tell you that is wrong. Yes, it is true that God wants us to remain steadfast; James 1:4 confirms it

[4]But let patience (steadfast) have its perfect work, that you may be perfect and complete, lacking nothing.

However, you must recognize that to be, "perfect and complete," time and maturity must happen first. Within being steadfast, there is growth. Don't believe that being stagnant is good, because it is only part of you completing the S.O.S. plan.

"O"

The second letter, *"O"* stands for Ongoing. This means to continue without interruption or distraction. Ongoing is good under normal circumstances, but dangerous when added with being Stagnant. If you don't work and progress towards a goal, your stagnant life will be an ongoing cycle until you make a change. Often, I hear people say, "I can't change," or "I can't do this without help." "I'm staying right here until God gives me a sign." Well, contrary to your belief, James 2:26 says,

26 For as the body without the spirit is dead, so faith without works is dead also.

The ongoing stagnation will remain dead and your goals, positive ideas, thoughts, and needs will never come to fruition. If you want to make money, then go work for it. If you want to put a ring on your lady's hand, then go buy the ring. If you smell foul, then take a shower and get clean. Remaining in an ongoing state will lead you to the last letter *"S"*.

"S"

The last letter *"S"* stands for S.I.N. Earlier, I placed "S.I.N." in quotation marks and mentioned that I would tell you why. This is the very crucial part of the S.O.S. plan, because once you learn and understand with the three areas combined, your thought process will guide itself out of the S.O.S. plan. If you look on the internet, you will find different acronyms for SIN such as "self-inactivating", "sinus", or a biblical favorite, "self-inflicting nonsense". I have created my own, so don't try to steal it, or I will be getting paid off you. My acronym for S.I.N. stands for, "Some Ignorant Nucklehead(s)". I know nucklehead is spelled Knucklehead, but that's the point. Why would you allow yourself to be that ignorant in your decision making where you don't even deserve the "K" in the word knucklehead". I talk with my brother everyday about his son and one day I said, "He is some ignorant knucklehead." When you continue to go down the wrong path over and over again, especially with clear knowledge of what damage that could happen, then you have become "Some Ignorant Nucklehead". If you are willing to combine these three areas into your life, you have graduated to completing the S.O.S. plan with a Stagnant Ongoing "S.I.N." degree; Proverbs 21:30 confirms it,

[30]There is no wisdom or understanding, Or counsel against the LORD.

S.O.S. PLAN EXAMPLES

Let's go over some examples of the S.O.S. plan that you may have experienced and learn why the S.O.S. plan will hinder growth and decision making.

S.O.S. PLAN #1- Academics

Having the, "Just Get It Done" attitude, I barely made it through to college. I was smart and had the capability of being at the top of my class, but did not apply myself. I was called stupid for most of my life and allowed it to be my dark cloud in school. This was my S.O.S. plan. I goofed off the first half of the semester and my grades would suddenly drop to D's and F's. I would work in overdrive the second half of the semester to bump up to a C, or possibly a B average. Now, what if I had applied myself way in the beginning of the semester? I probably would have gotten straight A's for the entire school year. The only A that was consistent was in Physical Education and that was due to my enjoyment of sports. I was almost expelled from school because of my dismal 2.2 G.P.A., but God had plans for me. Part of God's plan was marrying my wife. She has shown me how to work in excellence through organization. After that, the S.O.S. plan of academics was done. I had to make a choice. Either I lived a life of misdirection, or I'd live a life of direction and purpose. I was in the gray zone and believed I could cut corners and still pass. If we are to be Christ-like and ordained by God to work in perfection, then that is what we should strive for as it says in Matthew 5:48:

> *⁴⁸ Therefore you shall be perfect, just as your Father in heaven is perfect"*
>
> *Settling for less than who you are will not get it done.*

S.O.S. PLAN #2- Relationships

As a man, I thought my purpose was to sex every woman I encountered. Even after my spirit and gut feeling spoke, I continued to live ungodly. Part of my S.O.S. plan was to have sex with one girl from all the black sororities. If a girl told me that she was trying to live a godly life, I would purposely get them to have sex with me, so I could prove them wrong. I had been with multiple women just to say I had them. I'm sure you are thinking, "You are the man," but let's keep it real. Out of all these Stagnant Ongoing "S.I.N" moments that I thought were cool and praised for, I never bothered to think about the hurt that I was doing to the body God gave me. Besides possibly experiencing natural disasters like STIs, AIDS, and an unwanted, or unloved pregnancy, spiritually I was sharing a piece of my soul with another person that I was not connected to under God. Fellas, have you ever had sex with a virgin and noticed that the girl seemed extra clingy, or attached? It's not because you, "laid it down", it's because she gave up the purest connection God could give a woman. Fellas, stop passing it out like a business card. One day your Stagnant Ongoing "S.I.N." business will send you into bankruptcy. Genesis 19:1-29 speaks about the immoralities of Sodom and Gomorrah. It didn't end so well for them. Love or hate this story, the people had no problems with decision making. They decided to have all the sex they wanted and were proud of it. They epitomized the idea of Mind Interpretation Theory by making that choice, but in their wrong-doing, they all burned to the ground.

Ladies, your S.O.S. plan may include the same "S.I.N." behaviors as a man, but is done in a more cunning way. Men don't see the financial potential of giving up the "goods", you do and you are killing yourself just like men. If you are sexing men and giving your body, you are a prostitute. Now you're probably saying, "Hold up! Who you calling a prostitute?!" Let's look at three examples of a prostitute. Have you ever had sex with someone after they bought you dinner and drinks? Or maybe he purchased you clothes and to thank him you had sex with him? Well, that is a prostitute. Have you ever had sex with someone, because you felt bad for them or wanted to make them feel better? Again, that is a prostitute. Have you purposely gone out, saw a good-looking man and went to a motel, or took him home for a one night stand? Yup, that would be a prostitute. Prostitution is defined as the act of having sex in exchange for money, or the use of a skill, or ability in a way that is not appropriate, or respectable. You may not physically walk the streets at night, or work for an escort service, but the actions are still prostitution. I am not judging you, but if you are doing this, or have done this then consider yourself a prostitute. Men, we can consider ourselves prostitutes too. I can easily raise my hand because I was one. You can't be promiscuous and have a sexual drive motive and not see yourself as a prostitute. Or maybe you can, especially if you are living in the gray zone and accepting the S.O.S. plan of relationships. Ladies, you are a precious treasure. You are the giver of life; the mothers of our children. Without you, life would not exist. Why play yourself short? You are just as important as men. Better yourself by making the best choices for your life.

Micah 6:8

[8] He has shown you, O man, what is good; And what does the LORD require of you But, to do justly, to love mercy, And to walk humbly with your God or with God?

S.O.S. PLAN #3-The Conscious Unconscious

I know you are wondering what the "conscious unconscious" means, since they both have different meanings. Have you ever studied for a test, but still cheated? Did you go on a date with someone you didn't like, because you felt obligated to? Have you ever had sex with someone other than your spouse just to keep them quiet, because they were blackmailing you? These are few examples of the "conscious unconscious" idea within the S.O.S. plan. Compromising yourself and your values to please others is a bad decision. The Conscious Unconscious is another form of the gray zone. Your spirit tells you what you are supposed to do, but you do the complete opposite. This was a big part of my S.O.S. plan, because I thought I was supposed to be nice and giving. Yes, these attributes are good to have, but it should not compromise your morals. My conscious unconscious was to have sex, although I knew it was wrong. That decision not only hurt me spiritually, but the women I had sex with. The Bible teaches us to do for others, but I think we misinterpret the part that we should "do" others without thought. We have the heard the cliché of being "in our right mind", well if you're of God, your mind is right. James 3:13-18 speaks about heavenly (righteous decision) wisdom versus demonic (wrongful doing) wisdom.

13 Who is wise and understanding among you? Let him show by good conduct that his works are done in the meekness of wisdom.

14 But if you have bitter envy and self-seeking in your hearts, do not boast and lie against the truth.

15 This wisdom does not descend from above, but is earthly, sensual, demonic.

16 For where envy and self-seeking exist, confusion and every evil thing are there.

17 But the wisdom that is from above is first pure, then peaceable, gentle, willing to yield, full of mercy and good fruits, without partiality and without hypocrisy.

18 Now the fruit of righteousness is sown in peace by those who make peace.

This scripture explains how the "conscious unconscious" works within the S.O.S. plan. The will and wisdom to be righteous will govern your daily walk and lead you to making decisions that are not self-seeking. If you know it's wrong, then it's most likely wrong.

S.O.S. PLAN #4-Biblical Stupidity

This last example of the S.O.S. plan is based on biblical stupidity I have witnessed over the years. The lack of knowledge and wisdom always plays a major part in the S.O.S. plan. Over the years, I have heard some really asinine statements in the church. Some pastors, priests, and scholars have used a part of the Bible and misrepresented the message, or scripture's meanings. The Bible speaks about taking communion in 1 Cor. 11:23-34 which reads;

23 For I received from the Lord that which I also delivered to you: that the Lord Jesus on the same night in which He was betrayed took bread;

24 and when He had given thanks, He broke it and said, "Take, eat this is My body which is broken for you; do this in remembrance of Me."

25 In the same manner He also took the cup after supper, saying, "This cup is the new covenant in My blood. This do, as often as you drink it, in remembrance of Me."

26 For as often as you eat this bread and drink this cup, you proclaim the Lord's death till He comes.

27 Therefore whoever eats this bread or drinks this cup of the Lord in an unworthy manner will be guilty of the body and blood of the Lord.

28 But let a man examine himself, and so let him eat of the bread and drink of the cup.

29 For he who eats and drinks in an unworthy manner eats and drinks judgment to himself, not discerning the Lord's body.

30 For this reason many are weak and sick among you, and many sleep.

31 For if we would judge ourselves, we would not be judged.

32 But when we are judged, we are chastened by the Lord, that we may not be condemned with the world.

33 Therefore, my brethren, when you come together to eat, wait for one another.
34 But if anyone is hungry, let him eat at home, lest you come together for judgment. And
the rest I will set in order when I come.

Conclusion

For years, I was told that anyone who takes of the cup in an *"unworthy manner"* will *"become weak and sick, maybe die."* Those who believe this have to be on the S.O.S. plan. If you recall, Jesus shared the gospel, healed the sick and accepted mans' sins for them to live in eternity with the Father. The blood and bread are symbols of God's healing, right? Why would God send His only son to die on the cross and limit Himself to only those who are Christians? Jesus healed all, not just those who were Christians. The idea of *unworthy manner*, I believe references to those who completely don't care about the pain Jesus suffered to save our lives with complete disrespect. Offering someone the blood and bread is to promote healing for His children. When you accept Christ as your Lord and Savior your life will be enriched as a Christian. Imagine yourself at work. If you only do the bare minimum at your job, you get what you will receive. If you work above and beyond your responsibilities, you will receive more recognition and possibly more flexibility from your boss. God does not limit His blessings, but you can limit yourself from receiving them. I have seen children given the cup and was healed. They did not confess their life to Christ, but they were healed. Many think they cannot take of the cup and be healed. Believing those who are not Christians and in need of His healing cannot be healed, is nothing more than an S.O.S idea. I know my God heals all. It is acceptance of His son that we can have everlasting life and live life abundantly.

Breaking down the S.O.S. plan by each letter and providing examples was a way to help you recognize the S.O.S. plan in your life. These examples can be applied to family, church, friendship, or work. If there are other areas of your life where you are uncertain if the S.O.S. plan applies, just remember that God's word can answer your questions if you are willing to listen. To avoid the S.O.S plan, you must make careful and mature decisions with a righteous frame of mind.

S.O.S. plan = Give to receive.

Making the right choice = Give to be given.

S.O.S. plan = You wash my back, I'll wash yours.

Making the right choice = Wash the feet of others and seek nothing in return.

Proverbs 3:7-8

[7] *Do not be wise in your own eyes; Fear the* LORD *and depart from evil.*

[8] *It will be health to your flesh, And strength to your bones.*

Chapter Two...
S.O.S. Plan Reflection Exercise

Description of Exercise:

In chapter two, we begin to recognize that our decision making can improve by making rational, clear decisions. The idea was to recognize, witness, and accept those past decisions as being irrational, to also denying ever going back to making those same irrational decisions over again.

After reading chapter two, we are going to use this time to reflect on any personal findings about yourself and how you have gotten better. Each exercise will start with writing prayer/positive words of encouragement, and then followed by questions that reflect what you have read during this chapter. For this to work, you must be completely honest with what was learned and tell your truth. Remember, *I am all-knowing, but know-nothing;* you are in the position now to know all and leave past decisions of nothing behind.

1. Prayer/Positive words of encouragement

_____

_____

_____

_____

_____

2. Briefly define what S.O.S. plan means to you based on your understanding of chapter two?

_____

_____

_____

_____

3. What is or was a moment in life you felt the most stagnant? (Ex. job, relationship, church)

_____

_____

_____

_____

_____

_____

4. Based on the examples used in question 3. How long did you allow yourself to stay in that 'ongoing' situation?

_____

_____

_____

_____

_____

5. After answering question 2 and 3, when did you realize that you lived in "S.I.N."?

_____

_____

_____

_____

_____

_____

6. During the time of living life with an S.O.S. plan, how did you feel about yourself?

_____

_____

_____

_____

_____

_____

7. Since gaining understanding and moving from life in an S.O.S. plan, what is your thought process today?

_____

_____

_____

_____

_____

_____

8. Close with prayer/positive words of living life with direction

_____

_____

_____

_____

_____

_____

From knowing oneself to becoming intellectually sound; Twelve steps to keep you on the ground

CHAPTER Three...

SPIRITUAL DIRECTION OF REMOVING YOUR THEN, TO MOVING FORWARD TO NOW

Each person goes through several stages of growth. From the day of your birth, to the baby coos, to your first steps, to your first day of school, these are all part of the growth process. In chapter one, you were born into the world. We learned how to explore ourselves to gain the ability to shape our current state into a future of living righteous. In chapter two, we learned that the lack of knowledge and application prevented us from growing into our destined direction and everlasting existence. Now, it is time to move forward. Think about the following questions to give you spiritual direction to remove your then and move you to your now:

1. Are you a farmer that plant seeds with love?
Proverbs 19:8: "⁸He who gets wisdom loves his own soul;
He who keeps understanding will find good".

2. Are you farmer that plant seeds with discord?
Proverbs 19:9: "⁹A false witness will not go unpunished,
And he who speaks lies shall perish."

3. Are you farmer that tills the soil with no seeds?
Proverbs 19:10: "¹⁰Luxury is not fitting for a fool,
Much less for a servant to rule over princes."

Asking yourself these questions will allow you to think of what spiritual direction you are going in. Beginning with, "I am a farmer that plant seeds with love?" God teaches us to love our neighbor, brother, or sister in Romans 13:8, which says,

"⁸Owe no one anything except to love one another, for he who loves another has
fulfilled the law".

The first question is, *"Are you a farmer that plant seeds with love?"* God tells us that our belief in Him will cause us to love a person unconditionally and make wise decisions with a sound mind. The last two questions speak for themselves. If our thought process is, *"I do plant seeds with discord,"* then we might have missed something during our three, simple question evaluation. *Planting seeds with discord* means we are going throughout life without purpose, or understanding while instructing others what is best for them. That mission is to personally ruin someone else's life, because we choose to make costly decisions. Understand that *Discord* is defined as a conflict between things, or situations. In your case, it would be expecting yourself not to move forward. If you are a person who *till's the soil with no seeds,"* you are still working in the S.O.S. plan. Why would you spend hours upon hours tilling soil without any intentions of planting seeds? If you enjoy playing in dirt, then have at it, but you may need a reality check. If you feel you are continuing to live life as the farmer who plants seeds with discord, or tills the soil with no seeds, then you should go back to chapters one and two. Trust me, I had to repeat those chapters numerous times, because I did not have a clear understanding. Each day we grow and mature. By starting anew and making great, God-giving decisions you will become a better you.

During my journey my actions of *planting seeds with love* and my habits of making wise decisions changed for the better. Unfortunately, during this period of change, I struggled with communication. Communication is so important. It allows you to express your thoughts and feelings. I was afraid to share and tell the truth, because I allowed my life to control me. I read books with step by step programs on how to communicate, but the books did not offer God's truth to become a better person. As I started to *plant seeds with love* to reach my destiny, I became more open and forthcoming. I decided to write poetry, rap lyrics, letters, and stories. Those became my tool to feel comfortable in expressing my thoughts. During my personal journey, I finally found a way to leave my "then" and come into my "now." Then I had a sat back and stopped writing. I lost my confidence when I heard negative comments about my works. The negativity and opinion of others took me right back to "tilling the grounds with no seeds."

Today, I can look back and laugh at that time. I understand that my "now" is to thrive and prosper. My "then," was a blessing for me to experience *"tilling the grounds with no seeds."* It made me stronger and allowed me "to plant seeds with love by using God's words of wisdom. I needed to become a ruler within myself. To use God's word was like the constitution which helped me create my own government to lead me towards the truth about me. This allowed me to move towards my tomorrow.

Twelve steps to keep you grounded

I started this chapter by saying, *"From knowing oneself to becoming intellectually sound, Twelve steps to keep you grounded."* It is time for you to create your platform of inspirational words that will not only guide you daily, but for years to come. The number twelve in the title is very significant in the bible, which stands for ruler ship, government, and perfection. Here are some biblical examples of the number twelve's significance:

Mark 6:39-44

[39] Then He commanded them to make them all sit down in groups on the green grass. [40] So they sat down in ranks, in hundreds and in fifties. [41] And when He had taken the five loaves and the two fish, He looked up to heaven, blessed and broke the loaves, and gave them to His disciples to set before them; and the two fish He divided among them all. [42] So they all ate and were filled. [43] And they took up **twelve baskets** *full of fragments and of the fish. [44] Now those who had eaten the loaves were about five thousand men.*

The twelve tribes of Israel were considered the "perfection" of government and rule which is tribe was of the son of Jacob. Jacob was the man that wrestled to the break of dawn in Genesis 32:24-28

24 Then Jacob was left alone; and a Man wrestled with him until the breaking of day. 25 Now when He saw that He did not prevail against him, He touched the socket of his hip; and the socket of Jacob's hip was out of joint as He wrestled with him. 26 And He said, "Let Me go, for the day breaks." But he said, "I will not let You go unless You bless me!" 27 So He said to him, "What is your name?" He said, "Jacob." 28 And He said, "Your name shall no longer be called Jacob, but Israel; for you have struggled with God and with men, and have prevailed."

What is so great about the story of Jacob, the number 12 and the 12 tribes of Israel? As Jacob's name was changed to Israel, God's prophetic blessing by Israel name's sake means, "he who rules with God as a prince", "straight", "honest man of God" and/or "righteous man". These descriptions of Israel produced twelve children that were all a representative of government, perfection of God and ruler. Since we are descendants per say of Israel and he was a prince, that means you are now a King, or Queen of you. So, as you read Genesis 49:28:

*28 All these are the **twelve tribes of Israel**, and this is what their father spoke to them. And he blessed them; he blessed each one according to his own blessing.*

Those twelve tribes of Israel created a prosperous government which all came from one person, Jacob/Israel. Creating that government within yourself of righteous decisions can affect nations. Jacob/Israel did it, why can't we?

After reading chapters one and two, and learning the meaning of the number twelve biblically, this will help your life head towards your own perfection. By now, you have gained better understanding of oneself and is more intellectually sound of the truth about you. As you have learned the significance of the number twelve, I will leave you with my *Twelve Spiritual Direction of Inspirational Poetry, so you too can remove your THEN and move forward to NOW.* The direction portion of the twelve poems shows how each one is linked together, starting with prayer, to reaching destiny. By creating your own twelve inspirational words/poems and/or using what I have shared with you, you will have a daily, monthly, or yearly outlook of strengthening and trusting your decision making. I found it useful to write my own twelve inspirational words/poems instead of using someone else's work to express my truth, motivation, and understanding of me. What I have shared with you was based on the choices, growth, and prosperity for myself. What you might be led to write may be different as you write your own. I need you to really immerse yourself in the poems shared. These poems will be set from January through December, or whenever you get to the point of the book. The first poem should be read daily for the first month until you develop your own prayer. Then, for the second month, you will read poem number two and so on. Each poem is precisely set for each month, so you can grow your decision making and remain confident in completing your righteous direction. You can use these poems whenever, towards whatever, and however your time needs a spiritual uplifting. Take your time and enjoy this walk with God that He has blessed me with. Share it with loved ones as you will create your nation of persons making righteous decisions. After reading these twelve poems and in closing of the Truth chapters, we will be preparing for your graduation to learning how to perfect the trust within yourself.

Twelve Spiritual Direction of Inspiration

My Prayer

You: Lord Jesus Christ, please help me now. Every day I can feel my life going down.

Christ: I've been there for you since I've been around. Don't worry. You're my son, you're

heaven bound.

You: But Lord, please, tell me what I'm doing wrong. Every day I grow weaker and I'm not growing strong.

Christ: My son, just remember why you believe in me; that forever and a day, I will represent

thee. I know your trials get hard, tougher by the minute, but believing in me Yes! We can

deal with it.

You: But Lord, my thoughts, they can't be right. I think about sex and that fast-free life.

Christ: Son, that's the devil that wants your soul. You're not the only one in life that he has tried

to control. I will protect you today until the day you die. You

know, I am God, I will never lie.

Christ: Have I ever let you down?

You: No, you hooked me up.

Christ: So, why are you worried? As you say, you will stay jiggy. Don't worry about anything, or have any pity.

You: Thank you Lord God, I needed that inspiration. My mind's being refreshed in the Holy Ghost sensation.

Christ: If you ever need me again, just tap my hand. I will continue to do all I can.

You: Thank you Lord, you've done it again. Now, until the day I die, I will forever shout

AMEN!!!

Psalm 6:12

"⁴² For we do not wrestle against flesh and blood, but against principalities, against powers, against the rulers of the darkness of this age, against spiritual hosts of wickedness in the heavenly places."

Coming Home

Dear Lord, it is your child again. What am I doing wrong? What is it I need to do? My life is wonderful and I am thankful for that. What test am I going through? If there is a test, I need help passing, because I cannot do it alone. I thought maybe if I cheat a little bit, or ask for a hint my life would be easier, but I made it even harder. I love You Lord; please help me to be like you. I do not want to live here anymore. My friends say they like me and I do have a good time, but after my friends leave, I feel bad for hanging out with them. You blessed me with too much sometimes. I feel that I should give it back, because I do not deserve it. But you, Almighty Father, let me have these things in the grace of Your love for me. I love my toys, but my friends tell me to ask for more than what I did. I decided to ask for them, because I do not think it is right, but then my friends pitched in to get me those toys. I hope it is not too late for me to be raised some more by You, because You have always been there for me. Today is a new day and I promise not to be greedy, and listen to the friends You have given me and play with toys I already have. So, when You are ready Lord, just give me a call, because I am ready to Come Home.

2 Corinthians 5:1

"⁵For we know that if our earthly house, this tent, is destroyed, we have a building from God, a house not made with hands, eternal in the heavens."

Life is Not Over

At times, all good things may come to an end, but that does not mean Life is Over.

Certainly, when the body ceases itself from the dimension of society, the physical presence may ache with pain and tense itself with sorrow, but that Holy Ghost soul is waiting peacefully to witness true happiness.

What is written is not saying that time has come for the end, but for a new beginning. And remember where ever you go and whatever you do:

DO NOT BE AFRAID OF TOMORROW. GOD IS ALREADY THERE

John 11:25-26

"²⁵ Jesus said to her, "I am the resurrection and the life. He who believes in Me, though he may die, he shall live.

²⁶ And whoever lives and believes in Me shall never die…"

The Shadow of Christ

If the sun shines behind you would, Your shadow appears. The Life you walk may be a clean path to ecstasy, but it all actuality, it's on a road to destruction.

Finding a way to deliver oneself to a place only you can concede to is a step of witnessing happiness.

What is being contained in the mind may not be what is being contained in the heart.

Return to what creation has made you. Not far in distance will be the appearance of Your shadow.

Psalm 91:1-2

[1] He who dwells in the secret place of the Most High
Shall abide under the shadow of the Almighty.
[2] I will say of the LORD, "He is my refuge and my fortress;
My God, in Him I will trust."

It is in YOU

Society, Life, scared to live;

Jesus, Light, Forever in His will.

Women, Men, two to touch;

Wrapped in God's Holy Spirit will not do much.

Past, present, was scared to do;

Future, Forever; God's will is in YOU.

1 Corinthians 6:19-20

"19 Or do you not know that your body is the temple of the Holy Spirit who is in you, whom you have from God, and you are not your own?

20 For you were bought at a price; therefore, glorify God in your body and in your spirit, which are God's."

Enlighten Truth

The truth lights the darkness of all lies. Evil will continue to appear when those invite it.

The weight of a falsified life can get so heavy sometimes, you cannot control it.

Ways for peace is the truth.

Living for the world is being false.

Redirection, and intervention, could be a temporary answer for a life of lies, but only the Enlightened Truth will up root any evil destruction.

Ephesians 1:13-14

[13] *In Him you also trusted, after you heard the word of truth, the gospel of your salvation; in whom also, having believed, you were sealed with the Holy Spirit of promise,*

[14] *who is the guarantee of our inheritance until the redemption of the purchased possession, to the praise of His glory.*

Keeping ON

Straight ahead, and not aside; keep going forward, or you will fall behind.

If you look left, or maybe look right, your time will darken as eclipse at night.

Complete your goals and look ahead every day.

What is behind will slow you down, even a peak would turn you around.

Only forward in life is what I want for me and no one will come in the way of me, reaching destiny.

James 1:12

[12] *Blessed is the one who perseveres under trial, because having stood the test, that person will receive the crown of life that the Lord has promised to those who love him.*

Get Like Thee

God was first, no He is first; The One with might and superb talent enough to create life.

I look like Him, please; you've got to be kidding me.

He is God. I am man. I know God is too beautiful to look like me, walk like me, talk like me, especially think like me.

I know He would not be involved immorally like me, or continue to sin like me.

Wait a minute. Maybe the problem is that, I suppose to be like Him, not Him like me. Is there more for me to learn, or does this come naturally.

Ephesians 4:20-24

[20] But you have not so learned Christ,

[21] if indeed you have heard Him and have been taught by Him, as the truth is in Jesus:

[22] that you put off, concerning your former conduct, the old man which grows corrupt according to the deceitful lusts,

[23] and be renewed in the spirit of your mind,

[24] and that you put on the new man which was created according to God, in true righteousness and holiness.

I Wish

To each its own. You're not alone. Within my heart, you have a home.

The choices I make, sometime I will dislike, and without Your love, I will have restless nights.

Thank YOU for everything you've done; forever in my life, you will be #1.

I wish I may, I wish I might; that God will bless me with you another night.

John 15:7

"If you abide in me, and my words abide in you, ask whatever you wish, and it will be done for you."

Leave a Message

(Phone rings. No one answers, and the answering machine comes on.)

"I am sorry. I'm unable to accept your call, but leave a message and I will get back with you"

BEEP

(God leaves a message.)

"I remember when your message used to say, Thank you, and May God bless, but anyway..."

(God speaks on)

"Hey how are you doing? I have not heard from you in a while. I am upset that you have not called upon me in quite some time. Do not be afraid to say hi. I'm pleased to see everything is going well, but I know and feel that you still hurt inside. Do not forsake my help. I am there when things are good and I am good for you when things are bad. Just leaving a message. Call Me soon. I miss you. Your Father, Your Son, and Holy Spirit, God.

(Message ends. Answering machine is off.)

James 5:16

[16] *Confess your trespasses to one another, and pray for one another, that you may be healed. The effective, fervent prayer of a righteous man avails much."*

Whenever You Get This Message

Whenever you get this message; please raise your hands to the sky. With smile on face and with love in place; God is telling you Hi.

Don't forget your faith, your belief, and please don't forget your lunch. You see, each one will keep your mind, spirit, and body strong enough for that time of crunch.

Bills to pay, love gone astray, taking grief from people every day. Doesn't mean to quit, give up, or shut down, because things will be okay.

Whenever you do get this message, take it as Him slapping you with His hand. Not to hurt, but to help and just remember you are still within God's plan.

Deuteronomy 29:29

[29] *"The secret things belong to the LORD our God, but those things which are revealed belong to us and to our children forever, that we may do all the words of this law.*

Court in Session

Bailiff: "Here ye! Here ye! Case number 06/20/2009 is in order. This is case: Take two and call Him in the Morning.

Me: Your Honor, years ago, I committed myself to a lifestyle that is not even what it's supposed to be. Life was supposed to be glamorous, show-stopping, time consuming, and mesmerizing, but it's just a life. What do I suppose to get good from this?

Judge: Did you take an oath saying it was for better, or worse, sickness and health. Until death do you part?

Me: Yes, but I thought that was for marriage only.

Judge: Have you forgotten by taking oath, you are also under the Law of God?

Me: No sir

Judge: Have you kept my rules, thoughts, and Me first in all you do?

Me: No sir

Judge: Well before I sentence you, any last words?

Me: I want life sir, abundant life. I'm tired of wanting. I just want, I mean, I need to be better. I need you with me and in me. I need you to forgive me for all my wrong. I need you, Your Honor, to punish me accordingly.

Judge: Your judgment has sentenced you to be a Godly man, bound and covered by His grace and to follow the doctrine of God. If these things are not done, then His will, will not be done for you. And as far as your long journey, press forward and I love you. In Genesis 2:24, your separation to becoming one is life the joining of God, the Son, and the Holy Spirit; they can never be separated. As you are one, keep all deterrents away. And remember, I don't want to see you again in my courtroom, but if I do, I will love you unconditionally. Judgment is set at loving Him and having Christ in thee.

1 Corinthians 2:10-16

[10] *But God has revealed them to us through His Spirit. For the Spirit searches all things, yes, the deep things of God.*

[11] *For what man knows the things of a man except the spirit of the man which is in him? Even so no one knows the things of God except the Spirit of God.*

[12] *Now we have received, not the spirit of the world, but the Spirit who is from God, that we might know the things that have been freely given to us by God.*

[13] *These things we also speak, not in words which man's wisdom teaches, but which the Holy Spirit teaches, comparing spiritual things with spiritual.*

[14] *But the natural man does not receive the things of the Spirit of God, for they are foolishness to him; nor can he know them, because they are spiritually discerned.*

[15] *But he who is spiritual judges all things, yet he himself is rightly judged by no one.*

[16] *For "who has known the mind of the LORD that he may instruct Him?" But we have the mind of Christ.*

Conclusion of Truth: Book 1

These three chapters of learning your own individual Truth was rewarding, since it became more personal for you to know that your feelings about life, decision making, how God can be a blessing to you, and to know you are not alone. The poems of spiritual guidance that you can use monthly, daily, or forever, are the ones I still reference to occasionally. These are my true feelings that I expressed to you. Some inspirational books, poems, or thoughts are sometimes generated for entertainment, or money. What I have given you is a tool to remove any areas of "lack" and know that there is a light at the end of the tunnel. Or better yet, the light of God is with you when you think you are living in darkness. If you think about that in the natural sense; whenever you walk into a dark room or home before turning on the lights. Two different lights are activated.

1. Your eyes become adjusted to the darkness that surrounds you where you are able to feel your way to turn on the lights.

2. Your faithful sight is activated.

What is your faithful sight? Your faithful sight is when you can walk in darkness and know everything is in order and in place. Have you ever walked throughout your home without any lights on and made it to wherever you were going? If so you have that faithful sight that you know all is well and nothing will hinder you from moving forward. This faithful sight is the same in the spirit. Have you ever heard of, "walking by faith and not by sight?" Let's read 2 Corinthians 5:5-8

⁵ Now He who has prepared us for this very thing is God, who also has given us the Spirit as a guarantee.⁶ So we are always confident, knowing that while we are at home in the body we are absent from the Lord.⁷ For we walk by faith, not by sight. ⁸ We are confident, yes, well pleased rather to be absent from the body and to be present with the Lord.

Chapter Three...

Spiritual Direction of removing your THEN, to moving forward to NOW Reflection Exercise

Description of Exercise:

In chapter three, we begin the process of putting the past behind us and moving forward to the new life of truth. In this chapter, you were to find out who you are to yourself, knowing your decisions are made righteously, and accepting the truth based on clear evidence. No longer living in a gray area and accepting situations for what they are. You now have a better control of your own destiny to move forward in life. After reading chapter three, we are going to use this time to reflect on how you intend to move forward and remain growing in a positive direction. Each exercise will start with writing prayer/positive words of encouragement, and then followed by questions that reflect what you have read during this chapter. For this to work, you must be completely honest with what was learned and tell your truth. Remember, *from knowing oneself to becoming intellectually sound; twelve steps to keep you on the ground.*

1. Prayer/Positive words of encouragement

_____

_____

_____

_____

_____

_____

2. To remove yourself from the THEN to NOW, identify and check what type of farmer you are. Explain why?

- Are you a farmer that plant seeds with love? Proverbs 19:8
- Are you a farmer that plant seeds with discord? Proverbs 19:9
- Are you a farmer that tills the soil with no seeds? Proverbs 19:10

_____

_____

_____

_____

_____

_____

3. If you checked off either a *farmer with discord*, or *till the soil with no seeds* what are you currently doing to remain in either one of those areas?

_____

_____

_____

_____

_____

4. What could you do to change yourself to being a *farmer that plant seeds with love?*

_____

_____

_____

_____

_____

5. As a *farmer that plant seeds with love*, how many different ways can you be better at planting seeds?

_____

_____

_____

_____

_____

_____

6. The significance of twelve is to set a ruler ship, government, and make righteous decisions of truth within you. As mentioned during the chapter, I created twelve poems, or inspirational words that will direct the understanding of me and become stronger to meet my destiny.

I have provided twelve scriptures that correspond with my direction of truth, starting with a scripture of prayer to reach the destiny of recognizing the truth for what it will be. You can use my twelve directional poems to assist your walk of growth. I suggest you write your own twelve inspirational words that represent you. Reference back through Chapter three if you need to refresh your thoughts of the scriptures listed below. There is space provided to write your thoughts, but if you need more space, please write on a separate sheet of paper. This process should not be complete based on the space to write, but your feelings to produce your truth. If your thoughts are only eight words, to several pages, it will your true expression of writing that will set you up from your then and moving forward to your now.

Psalm 6:12

_____

_____

_____

_____

_____

_____

2 Corinthians 5:1

_____

_____

_____

_____

_____

John 11:25-26

_____

_____

_____

_____

_____

Psalm 91:1-2

_____

_____

_____

_____

_____

1 Corinthians 6:19-20

_____

_____

_____

_____

_____

_____

Ephesians 1:13-14

_____

_____

_____

_____

_____

_____

James 1:12

_____

_____

_____

_____

_____

_____

Ephesians 4:20-24

_____

_____

_____

_____

_____

_____

John 15:7

_____

_____

_____

_____

_____

James 5:16

_____

_____

_____

_____

_____

Deuteronomy 29:29

_____

_____

_____

_____

_____

1 Corinthians 2:10-16

_____

_____

_____

_____

_____

7. After discovering your twelve ways of inspiring your decision. What areas of your decision making you must work on the most?

_____

_____

_____

_____

_____

_____

8. Close with prayer/positive words of Truth

_____

_____

_____

_____

_____

Closure of Truth

Walking by faith, understanding and the TRUTH was what the first three chapters of this book were about. They were also about preparing, so you can have an understanding of oneself, becoming intellectually sound and on the ground. At some point of reading, I am sure you have asked, what is being on the ground? Being on the ground of which you stand on has you looking nowhere else but up. Through these chapters, we have built a *"foundation"* for you to move forward and feel confident with the truth of life. Having a foundation is pertinent to all our lives and it started by getting to know "you". Then you needed to gain the ability to remain directed in what you do and how you do it, to ending with a conclusion of removing your "then" and operating in the "now". Now that you have the foundation of truth set, it's time to move on to the next chapter, which is how to apply spiritual discernment to life in mind. But first, I must say to you, CONGRATULATIONS on your graduation. It is never easy to change who you are in a matter of three chapters, but I congratulate you on getting this far. We have move work to do. I want you to become so concrete in this that you can feel great confidence that your life won't turn backwards and you can go and help others as I have mentioned before. As we close these three chapters about TRUTH and we move on to the next book called, *How ONE Choice Directs Your Destiny: The Book of Trust Volume 2*

Let us give thanks for us coming this far together:

Dear Lord, we thank you for the wisdom you have given us thus far. It wasn't easy, but you have made a way. As you said in Job 28:10-11 [10] They tunnel through the rock; their eyes see all its treasures. [11] They search the sources of the rivers and bring hidden things to light." The foundation, the knowledge and understanding of You within us, was a mighty blessing to our lives. So, we thank you, we love you, and we adore. Now Lord as we move on to fulfill your greatness of trusting the spirit within us, stand with us in all that we do and that is IN JESUS NAME, AMEN!!!

Scriptural Index

Genesis 1:26..pg. 28

Genesis 1:27..pg. 27

Genesis 2:19-20..pg. 28

Genesis 2:24..pg. 66

Genesis 19:1-29..pg. 39

Genesis 32:24-28..pg. 52

Genesis 49:28..pg. 52

Exodus 3:9-15..pg. 24

Exodus 4:10-12..pg. 25

Leviticus…Numbers

Deuteronomy 29:29..pg. 65, 74

Joshua…Judges…Ruth…1 Samuel…2 Samuel…1 Kings…2 Kings…

1 Chronicles…2 Chronicles…Ezra…Nehemiah…Esther…

Job 28:10-11..pg. 77

Psalm 6:12..pg. 55, 72

Psalm 37:5..pg. 20

Psalm 91:1-2..pg. 58, 72

Proverbs 3:7-8..pg. 44

Proverbs 3:9-10..pg. 7

Proverbs 19:8..pg. 49

Proverbs 19:9..pg. 49

Proverbs 19:10..pg. 49

Proverbs 21:30..pg. 38

Ecclesiastes…SongofSolomon…Isaiah…Jeremiah…Lamentations…

Ezekiel…Daniel…Hosea…Joel…Amos…Obadiah…Jonah…

Micah 6:8..pg. 40

Nahum…Habakkuk…Zephaniah…Haggai…Zechariah…Malachi…

Matthew 5:48..pg. 39

Mark 6:39-44...pg. 51

Mark 11:24...pg. 18

Luke

John 10:10...pg. 14

John 11:25-26...pg. 57, 72

John 14:1-4..pg. 23

John 15:7..pg. 63, 74

Acts

Romans 13:8..pg. 49

1 Corinthians 2:10-16...pg. 66, 74

1 Corinthians 6:19-20...pg. 59, 73

1 Corinthians 11:23-34..pg. 42

2 Corinthians 5:1...pg. 56, 72

2 Corinthians 5:5-8...pg. 68

2 Corinthians 12:8-10...pg. 35

Galatians

Ephesians 1:13-14...pg. 60, 73

Ephesians 4:20-24...pg. 62, 73

Philippians...Colossians...1...Thessalonians...2Thessalonians...

1 Timothy...2 Timothy...Titus...Philemon...Hebrews...

James 1:4..pg. 36

James 1:12...pg. 61, 73

James 2:26...pg. 37

James 3:13-18..pg. 41

James 5:16...pg. 64, 74

1 Peter...2 Peter...1 John...2 John...3 John...Jude

Revelation 3:15-16..pg. 13

ABOUT THE AUTHOR

Dr. Edmond Kelly Jr. has worked in the education field for fifteen years, but truly gained knowledge and wisdom during his time as a young boy in ministry and through receiving his Masters of Counseling in 2012 and Doctoral degree in Educational Leadership in 2015 from Liberty University. As an author, his books, *How ONE Choice Directs Your Destiny*, is a self-inspirational book set as a three part series that prepares a person to learn about their *Truth*, *Trust* their decision making, and remaining in *Triumph* once they have overcome.

The book is also an introduction to his philosophy, *Mind Interpretation Theory*, which focuses on teaching how to make righteous decisions, which will help begin the process of working smart, not hard, and living a life in excellence.

He and his wife Felicia are blessed with two, beautiful children, Zoey and Elicia. He believes when making any decision, family should be the first thought in mind. He accredits his family as the guiding light to completing the book. As a philanthropist, author, and co-founder of Crossover Gear clothing line, he felt that education will be the driving force to bless others in need. Through counsel and mentorship, he has created developmental programs for youth, such as, Heroes Of Tomorrow youth ministry. He produced campaigns called the **BACK UP Plan**: *Bullying Awareness Constitute Knowledge & Ultimate Protection,* **Crossover Cares Foundation,** *which will create scholarships for college bound students, contributed to charities yearly,* and **Operation Save-A-Life.org** *that focuses on prevention of violence in the city of Chicago.* His passion for blessing others kept him grounded, humbled, and focused on making decisions to reach his own destiny, which is to give. *John 5:24 (NET)*

www.ingramcontent.com/pod-product-compliance
Lightning Source LLC
Chambersburg PA
CBHW062101280526
45788CB00003B/1311